Introduction

Welcome to this manuscript dedicated to maximizing business valuation with a focus on intangible assets! In this comprehensive book, we will delve into the intricacies and complexities that determine the value of a business. As an entrepreneur who has experienced a company's monetization, I have garnered valuable insights and knowledge, which I am thrilled to share with you in the pages ahead.

Business valuation is an essential process that seeks to determine the economic worth of a business or company. It is pivotal in numerous scenarios, such as mergers and acquisitions, raising capital, estate planning, and litigation. Understanding the factors that drive business valuation is vital for entrepreneurs, investors, and individuals involved in any aspect of finance.

Beyond the Balance Sheet

Throughout this book, we will examine the key factors that significantly influence business valuation. We will analyze not only the traditional tangible assets but also the often undervalued and intangible aspects of a business, such as goodwill, reputation, culture, and relationships. These elements play a crucial role in shaping the overall value of a business and can often be the deference between success and failure.

One of the most elusive yet valuable aspects of business valuation is goodwill. Goodwill encompasses the intangible assets and attributes of a company that contribute to its overall success and value. It goes beyond simply the assets listed on the balance sheet and includes factors such as customer loyalty, brand recognition, intellectual property, and even employee morale. Understanding how goodwill affects a business's valuation is essential, as it can significantly impact its market potential and attractiveness to potential investors or buyers.

Goodwill can be classified into two types: purchased goodwill and inherent goodwill.

Table Of Contents

Beyond the Balance Sheet

Beyond the Balance Sheet

Purchased goodwill refers to the value that is acquired when a business is purchased for more than its tangible assets. It represents the premium paid for intangible factors such as a well-established brand, a loyal customer base, or unique intellectual property. In contrast, inherent goodwill arises from factors that are developed and nurtured by the company over time, such as a positive company culture or strong employee relationships. Both types of goodwill contribute to the overall value of a business and must be carefully assessed during the valuation process.

Preserving goodwill during a sale transaction or change in ownership is a delicate process and requires careful consideration and planning. Potential buyers or investors often assess the continuity and transferability of goodwill when valuing a business. Maintaining consistent customer relationships, brand reputation, and employee morale are crucial factors in ensuring that goodwill remains intact and continues to contribute positively to the business's valuation.

Another crucial factor we will delve into is reputation. A business's reputation can be a double-edged sword, possibly elevating its value or tarnishing its chances of success. A solid and positive reputation enhances brand trust, customer loyalty, and market positioning, all of which directly influence the value of the business. Reputation also attracts investors, strategic partners, and talented employees, as they seek to align themselves with reputable organizations. Conversely, a damaged or negative reputation can erode trust and significantly devalue a company. Sustaining a positive reputation requires proactive management, consistent delivery of quality products or services, transparent communications, and ethical practices.

Culture, often underestimated in terms of its impact on business valuation, will also take center stage in this book. A company's culture refers to its shared values, beliefs, norms, and behaviors that shape the organization's identity and guide decisions and actions. A strong and aligned company culture can drive productivity, innovation, and employee satisfaction, ultimately leading to increased business value.

Beyond the Balance Sheet

Employees who resonate with the company's culture are more likely to be motivated, invested in the organization's success, and committed to delivering exceptional results. On the other hand, a poor or misaligned culture can hamper growth, weaken employee morale, erode trust, and negatively impact the bottom line. Investors and buyers consider company culture when evaluating potential acquisitions, as a positive culture contributes to the long-term sustainability and growth potential of the business.

Relationships, both within and outside the organization, will be thoroughly examined in the context of business valuation. Strong relationships with employees, customers, suppliers, and other stakeholders are fundamental to a company's success. Positive relationships with employees foster loyalty, engagement, and a sense of ownership in the company's success.

These factors, in turn, contribute to enhanced productivity and a collaborative work environment. Strong customer relationships lead to repeat business, brand advocacy, and increased market share.

Suppliers who trust and value their relationship with the company often provide preferential terms, reliable delivery, and access to innovative products or services. Cultivating and maintaining these relationships over time translates into a durable competitive advantage that adds significant value to the business.

Finally, we will explore the concept of a compelling vision and its impact on business valuation. A clear and inspiring vision not only guides the organization's strategic decisions but also attracts investors, strategic partners, and dedicated employees who share in that vision. A compelling vision provides a sense of purpose and direction, motivating stakeholders to invest their time, energy, and resources in the attainment of shared goals.

Investors seek companies with a strong vision as it demonstrates the potential for long-term growth and profitability. A visionary leader who effectively communicates and executes the company's vision can generate enthusiasm and loyalty from all stakeholders, elevating the business's value proposition.

Throughout this book, real-life examples and case studies will illustrate the concepts discussed. These examples will provide practical insights into how the factors we explore can have tangible implications on a business's value. We will analyze successful companies that have maximized their valuation potential through astute management of intangible assets, as well as cautionary tales of companies that neglected these critical factors to their detriment.

Whether you are an entrepreneur seeking to increase the value of your own company, an investor looking to make informed decisions, or an individual simply interested in understanding the dynamics of business valuation, this book will serve as a comprehensive guide. By the end of our journey together, you will understand how to maximize the value of your own business or make informed decisions as an investor, armed with a comprehensive knowledge of the factors that drive a company's worth.

Beyond the Balance Sheet

Kevin Brady

Understanding Business Valuation

Business valuation is a highly sophisticated and essential concept encompassing multiple dimensions in evaluating the economic worth of a company. This comprehensive assessment is instrumental in various scenarios, including mergers and acquisitions, financial planning, investment decisions, and legal disputes. Regardless of your role as an entrepreneur, investor, or professional, a deep understanding of business valuation is essential for making informed and strategic choices to maximize opportunities and minimize risks.

One of the most widely used approaches in business valuation is the financial valuation method. This method focuses on analyzing a company's historical financial performance, as well as projecting its future financial potential. Key financial indicators, such as revenue growth, profitability, cash flow patterns, and return on investment, are carefully examined to gauge a company's overall financial stability and growth prospects.

Understanding these financial aspects helps stakeholders assess the risks associated with investing or partnering with a company and forecast future returns.

Another key method used in business valuation is the market valuation approach. This approach involves assessing a company's value by comparing it to similar businesses within the industry. By analyzing market multiples such as the price-to-earnings (P/E) ratio, price-to-sales (P/S) ratio, or price-to-book (P/B) ratio, practitioners gain insights into how the market values comparable companies. This allows for a better understanding of investor sentiment, industry trends, and the potential value range for the subject company. The market valuation approach is particularly useful when evaluating companies operating in well-defined industries with established benchmarks and when assessing market sentiment towards a specific sector.

Beyond the Balance Sheet

In addition to financial and market-based approaches, the asset-based valuation method considers a company's tangible and intangible assets as well as liabilities. Tangible assets encompass physical items, such as land, buildings, machinery, and inventory, while intangible assets include intellectual property, brand value, customer relationships, and goodwill. This method is particularly applicable to businesses where physical assets play a significant role or in industries where intangible assets significantly contribute to a company's value. By assessing these assets and liabilities, practitioners can better understand a company's underlying value beyond just its financial performance or market position.

It is important to note that each valuation method has its own strengths and weaknesses and may be more appropriate depending on the specific circumstances. In many cases, combining techniques provides a comprehensive view of a company's value, considering its financials, market comparables, and underlying assets.

Beyond the Balance Sheet

Understanding business valuation holds paramount importance for several reasons. Firstly, it empowers investors and entrepreneurs to make informed decisions when evaluating investment opportunities. By diligently analyzing a company's financial performance, market positioning, and growth potential, stakeholders can assess the associated risks and rewards and make well-founded investment choices.

Moreover, business valuation plays a crucial role in determining a fair selling price for a business during a merger, acquisition, or succession planning process. By obtaining a realistic understanding of a company's worth, sellers can engage in negotiations with potential buyers more effectively, ensuring a fair and equitable transaction for both parties involved.

Furthermore, business valuation is invaluable for attracting potential investors or securing financing for business expansion. By presenting a comprehensive valuation report to potential investors or lenders, entrepreneurs can demonstrate the attractiveness of their business and justifiably request the desired capital injection.

Beyond the Balance Sheet

Additionally, business valuation aids in assessing the overall financial health and performance of a company. By analyzing key financial metrics and comparing them to industry benchmarks, stakeholders can identify areas for improvement and develop strategic initiatives accordingly. This understanding of a company's value helps stakeholders implement measures aimed at enhancing competitiveness, profitability, and long-term sustainability.

Beyond financial factors, business valuation also takes into account qualitative aspects that significantly impact a company's value. These include factors such as the company's reputation, brand strength, customer loyalty, quality of management, and employee morale.

Assessing these qualitative factors provides a deeper understanding of a company's position in the market and its potential for growth and value creation.

In summary, comprehending business valuation is essential for navigating the intricate world of business. Its application spans from investment decisions to financial planning and legal disputes. By gaining a comprehensive understanding of the methodologies and factors that drive business valuation, stakeholders can synergize their analytical skills and make well-informed decisions in the dynamic and competitive business landscape.

In the subsequent chapters, we will delve even deeper into the factors that drive business valuation, exploring concepts such as intangible assets, risk analysis, industry dynamics, and market positioning. By gaining a more profound understanding of these factors, stakeholders can elevate their valuation analyses and make even more informed and accurate decisions, positioning themselves as knowledgeable and successful entrepreneurs or investors.

Factors that Drive Valuation

When it comes to valuing a business, there are numerous factors that come into play.

Understanding these factors is crucial for both buyers and sellers, as they can determine the worth and potential of a business. In this chapter, we will delve into the key factors that drive business valuation.

1. Financial Performance

Financial performance is a primary factor in determining a business's value. It thoroughly assesses the company's historical and projected revenue, profitability, cash flow, and growth potential. Buyers are keen on acquiring businesses that demonstrate consistent financial performance, as it provides assurance of the company's ability to generate profits and repay investments.

Beyond the Balance Sheet

Revenue: The revenue generated by a business is a critical factor to consider. Buyers examine the sources of revenue and assess their sustainability. Are they diversified across different customer segments, products, or geographical locations? Furthermore, buyers analyze the profitability of each revenue stream to understand their contribution to the business's overall financial health. Additionally, revenue growth rates and historical patterns help evaluate the potential for future revenue generation.

Profitability: Beyond revenue, profitability is a key indicator of a company's financial health.

Profit margins, such as gross profit margin and net profit margin, are analyzed to determine if the business operates efficiently and has the ability to generate profits after covering costs. Buyers look at the consistency of profit margins over time and compare them to industry benchmarks to assess the company's competitiveness and its potential for sustained profitability and growth.

Cash Flow: Cash flow represents the amount of cash generated or used by a business over a specific period. Positive cash flow indicates that a business is generating more cash than it is spending, enhancing its valuation. Buyers analyze the company's operating, investing, and financing activities to gauge its cash flow's sustainability and quality. They also consider the cash flow conversion cycle, which measures the time it takes for a company to convert its investments in inventory and other resources into cash.

Growth Potential: Buyers are always interested in the growth potential of a business.

Assessing growth potential involves evaluating industry trends, market demand, customer preferences, and the company's ability to adapt and innovate. Market research, competitor analysis, and customer surveys help determine if a business is well-positioned to capitalize on future growth opportunities. Buyers also consider factors such as the scalability of the business model, expansion plans, and the potential for mergers and acquisitions.

Cash Flow: Cash flow represents the amount of cash generated or used by a business over a specific period. Positive cash flow indicates that a business is generating more cash than it is spending, enhancing its valuation. Buyers analyze the company's operating, investing, and financing activities to gauge its cash flow's sustainability and quality. They also consider the cash flow conversion cycle, which measures the time it takes for a company to convert its investments in inventory and other resources into cash.

Growth Potential: Buyers are always interested in the growth potential of a business.

Assessing growth potential involves evaluating industry trends, market demand, customer preferences, and the company's ability to adapt and innovate. Market research, competitor analysis, and customer surveys help determine if a business is well-positioned to capitalize on future growth opportunities. Buyers also consider factors such as the scalability of the business model, expansion plans, and the potential for mergers and acquisitions.

2. Market Conditions

Market conditions have a significant impact on business valuation. The overall state of the economy, industry trends, market demand, and competitive landscape play crucial roles. A business operating in a growing and lucrative market will likely have a higher valuation than a declining or saturated market.

Industry Trends: Buyers assess the current and future trends within the industry in which the business operates. This includes understanding factors such as technological advancements, regulatory changes, shifting consumer preferences, and emerging markets. A business that is well-positioned to capitalize on these trends is considered more valuable. For instance, with the rise of e-commerce, businesses with a strong online presence and efficient logistics capabilities may be valued higher.

Market Demand: The demand for a business's products or services is a critical factor when determining its value. Buyers analyze factors such as customer demographics, market size, and potential for expansion. A business with a strong customer base and high demand for its offerings is likely to have a higher valuation. Additionally, buyers assess the competitive landscape and consider if the business has a unique value proposition that differentiates it from competitors and attracts customers.

Competitiveness: The competitive landscape within an industry is crucial in assessing business valuation. Buyers evaluate the strength of a business's competitors, their market share, and the level of market concentration. A business that has managed to differentiate itself and gain a competitive advantage is more likely to be valued higher. This could be achieved through factors such as product innovation, superior customer service, cost leadership, or strong brand recognition.

Economic Climate: The overall economic conditions, such as inflation rates, interest rates, and unemployment rates, can influence business valuation. In a strong and stable economy, buyers may be willing to pay a premium for businesses with growth potential. Conversely, business valuations may be affected in an economic downturn as buyers become more cautious. The economic climate's stability and predictability impact the perceived risk level associated with the business.

3. Tangible and Intangible Assets

The assets a business possesses are key considerations in determining its value. Assets can be classified as tangible or intangible, with both types contributing to the overall valuation.

Tangible Assets: Tangible assets include physical properties, equipment, inventory, and real estate owned by the business.

Buyers consider the condition and value of these assets, as they can directly contribute to future revenue generation or be sold to generate additional cash flow. Having well-maintained and up-to-date tangible assets adds value to a business. For example, a manufacturing company with state-of-the-art production facilities and modern equipment may be valued higher than one with outdated technology.

Intangible Assets: Intangible assets are non-physical assets that can significantly impact a business's value. These include intellectual property, trademarks, patents, brand reputation, customer relationships, and proprietary technology. Intangible assets are often critical to a business's competitive advantage and ability to differentiate itself. Buyers consider the strength and protection of these assets when valuing a business. For instance, a software company with a portfolio of patented technology and a recognizable brand name may be valued higher due to the intellectual property it possesses.

Intellectual Property: Intellectual property, such as patents, copyrights, and trade secrets, can enhance a business's valuation. Patents grant exclusive rights to an invention and can provide a competitive advantage. Buyers assess the strength and validity of intellectual property rights and evaluate their potential to generate future revenue. They also consider the potential for licensing or selling the intellectual property to other companies.

Brand Reputation: A strong brand reputation is an intangible asset that can contribute significantly to a business's value. Buyers consider factors such as brand recognition, customer loyalty, and brand equity when assessing a business's valuation. A well-established brand with a positive reputation can attract a larger customer base and command premium pricing. Buyers also assess the brand's ability to extend into new markets and its alignment with current market trends and customer preferences.

Customer Relationships: The quality and strength of customer relationships are valuable intangible assets. Buyers analyze customer retention rates, satisfaction levels, and the overall customer base to assess the potential for future revenue generation. A business with a loyal customer base and long-term customer relationships is often valued highly. Buyers also consider the level of customer diversification to ensure that the business is not overly reliant on a small number of key customers, mitigating the risk of revenue loss.

4. Industry and Company Positioning

The position a business holds within its industry can greatly impact its valuation. A company with a competitive advantage, unique market positioning, or a strong market share is likely to be valued higher than its peers.

Competitive Advantage: Buyers evaluate the business's competitive advantage, which could stem from factors such as unique products or services, cost leadership, or technological innovation. A competitive advantage allows a company to outperform its competitors and achieve higher profitability. Businesses with sustainable competitive advantages are often valued more favorably. For example, a company that has developed a proprietary technology or a well-recognized brand may have a competitive advantage over its rivals and therefore have a higher valuation.

Market Share: A business's market share within its industry is essential in determining its value. Buyers consider the size and growth potential of the market, as well as the business's market share relative to its competitors. A business with a significant market share may be seen as a leader in its industry and, therefore, have a higher valuation.

Additionally, a strong market position allows a business to negotiate better terms with suppliers, attract top talent, and gain customer loyalty.

Market Positioning: How a business positions itself in the market is also crucial in determining its value. Buyers assess factors such as the target market, pricing strategy, distribution channels, and branding to understand how customers perceive the business and how it differentiates itself from competitors. A company that has successfully positioned itself as offering unique value to customers may command a higher valuation.

For example, a luxury brand that appeals to a niche market and commands premium pricing may be valued higher than a mass-market brand.

5. Management Team and Human Capital

The management team and employees of a business are integral to its success and can impact its valuation. Buyers consider the experience, expertise, and track record of the management team in driving growth and managing the business effectively.

Management Team: The capabilities and experience of the management team are key considerations in determining the value of a business. Buyers assess the qualifications and track record of key executives, their ability to lead the company, and their strategic vision. A strong management team with a proven track record of delivering results and driving growth is often valued more favorably. Buyers also consider the depth of the management team and the presence of succession plans to ensure the continuity of leadership.

Key Employees: The strength and expertise of the employees, particularly key employees, are important factors in business valuation. Buyers assess the knowledge and skills of employees, especially those who play a critical role in the success of the business. Key employees may have unique industry insights, customer relationships, or specialized technical knowledge that adds value to the business. Buyers also consider employee retention rates and the presence of non-compete agreements to mitigate the risk of key employees leaving after the acquisition.

6. Risk Factors

Risk factors associated with a business can impact its valuation. Buyers assess the level of risk and uncertainties involved in acquiring and operating the business.

Industry Risks: Buyers evaluate the specific risks associated with the industry in which the business operates. This includes regulatory changes, technological disruptions, competitive pressures, and market volatility. Companies operating in highly regulated industries or those that are heavily dependent on a single customer or supplier may carry higher risk. Buyers consider the potential impact of these risks on the business's financial performance and growth potential.

Financial Risks: Financial risks, such as excessive debt, liquidity constraints, and poor financial management, can affect a business's valuation. Buyers assess the financial health and stability of the business, including its debt-to-equity ratio, interest coverage ratio, and cash flow management. Businesses with strong financial controls, healthy cash flow, and manageable debt levels are often valued higher.

Legal and Regulatory Risks: Legal and regulatory risks, such as pending litigation, compliance issues, and intellectual property disputes, can impact business valuation. Buyers conduct due diligence to identify any potential legal or regulatory problems that could affect the business's operations or reputation. The presence of clear and valid legal contracts, intellectual property protection, and compliance with applicable regulations can enhance a business's value.

Conclusion

Valuing a business is a complex process that takes into account numerous factors. Financial performance, market conditions, tangible and intangible assets, industry and company positioning, management team and human capital, and risk factors determine business valuation. Buyers and sellers should thoroughly analyze these factors to arrive at a fair and accurate valuation that reflects the true worth and potential of the business.

Beyond the Balance Sheet

30

Unveiling the Importance of Goodwill

Goodwill is frequently mentioned in the business world, yet its significance is often underestimated or misunderstood. Beyond tangible assets and financial statements, goodwill represents a business's intangible value. It encompasses factors such as brand reputation, customer loyalty, employee morale, and relationships with suppliers and stakeholders, playing a crucial role in determining the overall value and potential of a company.

Goodwill extends beyond the realm of customers. A business's relationships with its suppliers, partners, and stakeholders are crucial for success. These relationships are based on trust, reliability, and mutual benefit. A company with solid goodwill is often given preferential treatment, resource access, and better terms from suppliers, enhancing its competitive advantage. Moreover, stakeholders are more likely to support a business with a positive reputation, reinforcing the importance of goodwill in attracting investment, partnerships, and collaboration.

Kevin Brady

Internal goodwill, encompassing employee morale and motivation, is another vital aspect to consider. A positive work culture, where employees feel valued, encouraged, and engaged, fosters productivity and innovation. Engaged employees are more likely to go above and beyond, leading to increased efficiency and eventually, improved profitability. They become strong advocates for the company, positively impacting both internal operations and external branding efforts.

In addition to impacting day-to-day operations, goodwill plays a significant role in business valuation. Prospective buyers or investors closely evaluate the goodwill of a company, understanding its potential for long-term success and profitability. A business with a vital goodwill factor becomes an attractive investment opportunity, often receiving higher offers and securing better deals during a sale or merger. Goodwill, therefore, has a direct impact on the financial worth of a company.

However, to fully comprehend the importance of goodwill, it is essential to delve deeper into its various dimensions. One such dimension is social responsibility. In today's society, businesses are increasingly expected to act in socially responsible ways, addressing environmental, social, and governance (ESG) issues. Companies that proactively engage in corporate social responsibility initiatives and align their values with the expectations of society are more likely to generate positive goodwill. They are perceived as ethical, trustworthy, and values-driven, earning the respect and admiration of customers, employees, and stakeholders.

It is important to note that these efforts should be considered complementary and not distract the organization's core mission; otherwise, other competitive advantages that increase enterprise value may be eroded.

Moreover, the digital age has transformed the dynamics of goodwill, amplifying its significance and impact.

Beyond the Balance Sheet

Online and social media platforms have provided customers powerful tools to express their opinions and influence others. A negative review or a viral social media incident can cause substantial harm to a business's reputation. Conversely, positive online engagement and word-of-mouth recommendations can propel a company's brand and goodwill to new heights. Therefore, businesses must actively monitor and manage their online presence, staying vigilant about customer sentiment and responding promptly and effectively to online interactions to protect and enhance their goodwill.

Another aspect worth considering is the role of leadership in building and maintaining goodwill. Leaders' actions and decisions significantly influence a company's overall perception. Ethical leadership practices, transparent communication, and a commitment to values-based decision-making demonstrate integrity and contribute to the goodwill of a business.

Beyond the Balance Sheet

Leaders who prioritize the well-being of their employees, foster a diverse and inclusive work environment and actively engage in community initiatives further enhance the goodwill of their organizations.

It is essential to recognize that goodwill is not a static concept; rather, it requires continuous investment and nurturing. Businesses must prioritize building and maintaining strong relationships with their stakeholders, investing in brand reputation through marketing, public relations, and customer service efforts, and fostering a positive and inclusive work culture.

By continuously cultivating goodwill, businesses can strengthen their position in the market, enhance their reputation, and secure long-term success.

Beyond the Balance Sheet

In conclusion, the depth and significance of goodwill in the business world become evident when exploring its various dimensions. Beyond customer loyalty, goodwill encompasses a company's relationships with suppliers, stakeholders, and employees. It also extends to social responsibility, online reputation management, and leadership practices. Recognizing and investing in goodwill is vital for businesses to thrive in an increasingly competitive landscape, as it enhances brand reputation, attracts customers and stakeholders, improves financial valuation, and contributes to long-term success.

Nurturing Your Reputation

In today's highly competitive business landscape, a company's reputation is a valuable asset that can greatly influence its success. A solid and positive reputation not only helps in attracting customers but also impacts the perceptions of investors, employees, and other stakeholders. It becomes imperative for businesses to understand the significance of safeguarding and nurturing their reputation.

Building a strong reputation begins with a clear understanding of the organization's values and mission. These core principles should serve as guiding lights, inspiring every decision and action taken within the company. By aligning business practices with these values, a company creates a consistent identity that resonates with customers and earns their trust.

This foundation of trust establishes a competitive advantage, potentially differentiating the company from its competitors.

Beyond the Balance Sheet

Transparency is another crucial element in nurturing reputation. Operating with openness and honesty in all interactions, both internally and externally, establishes credibility and builds a loyal customer base. When customers perceive a company as truthful and reliable, they are more likely to engage with its products or services. Transparency also extends to internal operations, including how decisions are made and how employees are treated.

When employees feel valued and informed, their commitment and loyalty to the company grow, enhancing the company's reputation both internally and externally.

Maintaining a robust online presence is essential for reputation management in the digital age. Today, the internet serves as a powerful medium allowing information to spread rapidly. Companies must proactively monitor and manage their online reputation, as it directly influences how customers and stakeholders perceive them. Staying informed about what is being said about the company across various online platforms enables timely responses and proactive engagement.

Beyond the Balance Sheet

Companies should implement tools to manage their online reputation effectively, such as social media monitoring and online sentiment analysis. These tools allow businesses to track mentions, reviews, and feedback about their products, services, and brand. By leveraging this information, they can identify potential issues and take swift action to address concerns or negative sentiments. Responding promptly to dissatisfied customers or negative reviews can help mitigate potential damage and demonstrate a commitment to customer satisfaction.

Furthermore, nurturing a positive reputation involves being socially responsible. Consumers increasingly expect companies to act in an ethical and sustainable manner. Aligning business practices with social and environmental values not only benefits society but also enhances a company's brand image. By practicing responsible sourcing, implementing sustainable production methods, and minimizing the company's ecological footprint, a company establishes itself as a responsible corporate citizen.

Beyond the Balance Sheet

Participating in philanthropic efforts, supporting meaningful causes, and giving back to communities also showcase the company's commitment to making a positive impact on society. Such efforts not only enhance reputation but also foster the loyalty and trust of customers who appreciate and align with the company's values. Engaging with stakeholders through corporate social responsibility initiatives can create opportunities for collaboration and foster positive relationships with the community, customers, and employees.

In addition to these efforts, building strategic partnerships and collaborations with other reputable organizations can also contribute to enhancing a company's reputation. By associating with established and respected partners, a company gains credibility and expands its reach. These partnerships can provide unique opportunities for knowledge sharing, innovation, and joint marketing efforts, all of which contribute to a positive reputation.

Beyond the Balance Sheet

Engaging in industry associations, participating in conferences and events, and fostering relationships with key influencers can further solidify the company's reputation as a thought leader and industry expert. Thought leaders are often sought after for insights and perspectives, and being recognized as one can lead to increased visibility, credibility, and influence. Sharing expertise through speaking engagements, publishing articles, or hosting webinars are avenues companies can explore to establish themselves as trusted authorities within their respective fields.

It is important to note that reputation management is an ongoing process, requiring constant vigilance and effort to safeguard and nurture. In a world where information is readily accessible, reputation can be both fragile and susceptible to negative sentiments.

Companies must remain attentive to the needs and expectations of their stakeholders, continuously improving their products and services, and making efforts to surpass customer expectations.

Taking proactive steps to address any negative feedback swiftly and efficiently can help mitigate potential damage to the company's reputation. Companies can adopt a proactive crisis management strategy, outlining procedures and communication plans to respond quickly and effectively to any reputational challenges that may arise. This preparedness allows companies to address crises promptly, demonstrate responsibility, and regain trust.

A positive reputation not only attracts customers but also helps in weathering challenges, gaining investor confidence, and fostering a positive work culture. Employees are more likely to feel proud of their association with a company that values its reputation, resulting in increased productivity and employee retention. Additionally, a strong reputation can open doors to new business opportunities, as partners and investors are more inclined to collaborate with a company they perceive favorably.

Beyond the Balance Sheet

Nurturing reputation becomes the cornerstone of business success. By building a clear and credible identity, promoting transparency, actively managing their online presence, practicing social responsibility, forming strategic partnerships, and establishing thought leadership, a company can cultivate a strong reputation that serves as a solid foundation for growth and sustainability.

In an era where reputation can make or break a business, investing in its nurturing is an essential endeavor for long-term success. By adopting a proactive mindset, understanding the impact of reputation across all areas of the business, and continuously monitoring and improving reputation management strategies, companies can build and maintain a positive reputation that fuels growth, enhances trust, and sets them apart in a competitive marketplace.

44

The Role of Culture

Culture plays a significant and multifaceted role in the overall valuation of a business. While financials and tangible assets are essential, intangible aspects, such as culture, can greatly influence a business's value. In today's globalized world, where companies are increasingly interconnected, understanding and managing cultures is vital for long-term success.

Culture refers to the shared beliefs, values, and practices that shape the behavior of individuals within an organization. It encompasses the way people communicate, make decisions, and collaborate. A strong and positive culture can have numerous benefits for a business, including improved employee morale, increased productivity, and enhanced customer satisfaction.

Beyond the Balance Sheet

When assessing the value of a business, potential investors or buyers consider the cultural aspects carefully. They recognize that a company with a healthy and thriving culture is more likely to have a loyal and motivated workforce. This, in turn, leads to improved employee retention rates and reduced recruitment and training costs. Moreover, a positive work environment is attractive to job seekers, allowing the company to attract top talent and facilitating innovation and creativity within the organization.

On the other hand, a toxic or dysfunctional culture can have a detrimental impact on business valuation. A culture marked by distrust, poor communication, and lack of accountability can lead to reduced productivity and increased employee turnover. This can result in higher costs for the company as they have to constantly recruit and train new employees. Additionally, a negative company culture can damage its reputation, making it harder to attract customers or retain existing ones.

Beyond the Balance Sheet

Assessing culture during the valuation process involves understanding the values and beliefs that underpin the organization's operations. It requires evaluating the alignment between the stated values and the actual behavior exhibited within the company. This can be done through interviews, surveys, and observation of the organization's day-to-day operations.

Cultural due diligence is an essential step that potential acquirers undertake to gain insight into the target company's culture. This includes understanding how cultural factors impact the company's performance, employee satisfaction, and business relationships. It examines the organization's leadership style, communication channels, decision-making processes, and the level of employee engagement. Moreover, cultural due diligence considers the compatibility of the target company's culture with the acquiring company's culture, as a lack of alignment can lead to integration challenges and hinder post-merger success.

Initiatives focused on improving culture, such as employee engagement programs, can yield significant benefits for both the employees and the business. For example, creating cross-functional teams and promoting collaboration can enhance innovation and problem-solving capabilities, improving productivity and a better overall performance.

Additionally, nurturing a culture of continuous learning and development can empower employees, positioning the company as an attractive place to work and enhancing its reputation as an employer of choice.

Leaders and managers play a critical role in shaping and fostering a positive culture. They need to ensure that the organization's values are consistently communicated and reinforced and that employees are held accountable for upholding these values. Effective leadership involves leading by example, demonstrating the desired behaviors through their actions, and providing support and resources to facilitate a positive work environment.

Leaders who embrace and embody the desired culture create a sense of purpose, inspire employees, and cultivate a strong organizational identity.

Furthermore, diversity and inclusion are important aspects of organizational culture that can contribute to business valuation. Embracing diversity in all its forms, including gender, ethnicity, age, and background, can lead to a more inclusive culture where diverse perspectives are valued, and innovation thrives. Studies have shown that diverse teams outperform homogeneous ones, leading to better decision-making, increased creativity, and ultimately, improved financial performance. A culture that celebrates diversity sends a positive message to customers, stakeholders, and the wider community, which can enhance brand reputation and support sustainable growth.

Beyond the Balance Sheet

Ultimately, culture has a direct impact on a company's reputation, customer perception, and financial performance. A strong culture can differentiate a business from its competitors and attract loyal customers who value the company's ethos. It can also increase brand equity, ultimately contributing to higher profitability and market value. Conversely, a negative culture can tarnish a company's image, affect customer loyalty, and erode its market position.

Business valuation requires a holistic understanding of both financial and non-financial factors, with culture playing a pivotal role. By recognizing the importance of culture and actively working to nurture a positive and supportive environment, businesses can enhance their value and position themselves for long-term success in an increasingly competitive marketplace. Effective leadership, embracing diversity and inclusion, and continuously investing in the development of employees are essential steps in creating a culture that adds value to the business and drives sustainable growth.

Cultivating Strong Relationships

In today's dynamic and interconnected business landscape, establishing and nurturing strong relationships has become a critical strategic imperative. Building long-term, mutually beneficial partnerships goes beyond mere transactions; it involves creating an ecosystem of trust, collaboration, and shared value. In this extended chapter, we will delve deeper into the key elements and strategies involved in cultivating strong business relationships and maximizing their value.

1. Understanding the Importance of Business Relationships

Strong business relationships form the foundation for success in any industry. They provide opportunities for knowledge-sharing, resource allocation, and joint problem-solving.

Moreover, these relationships foster loyalty, repeat business, and referrals, giving companies a competitive edge. Recognizing the intrinsic value of business relationships builds the motivation and commitment needed to develop effective strategies.

Developing meaningful connections and nurturing relationships with stakeholders takes time and effort, but the rewards are immense. By investing in these relationships, businesses create a robust network of allies who can open doors to new opportunities, provide critical insights, and offer unwavering support during challenging times.

2. Identifying Key Stakeholders

When developing a robust business relationship strategy, it is crucial to identify the key stakeholders involved. These stakeholders can be categorized into different groups, including clients, suppliers, employees, investors, regulators, and industry influencers. Each group plays a unique role in shaping the success of a business and requires tailored relationship-building efforts.

Beyond the Balance Sheet

Clients are the lifeblood of any organization, and understanding their needs, preferences, and pain points is paramount. By establishing a strong rapport with clients, businesses can anticipate their requirements, tailor their offerings to meet those needs, and ultimately build customer loyalty.

Suppliers are critical partners in the supply chain, and nurturing strong relationships with them ensures a steady and reliable flow of resources. Collaborating closely with suppliers facilitates effective inventory management, timely delivery schedules, and mutually beneficial negotiations.

Employees are the driving force behind any successful business. Building strong relationships with employees fosters a positive work environment, promotes loyalty, and enhances productivity. By valuing their contributions, providing growth opportunities, and actively listening to their concerns, businesses can cultivate a dedicated and talented workforce.

Investors and shareholders provide the necessary capital and support for business growth.

Nurturing strong relationships with these stakeholders involves transparent communication, demonstrating resilience during challenging times, and delivering long-term value that aligns with their financial goals.

Regulators play a crucial role in ensuring compliance and upholding ethical standards within industries. Building strong relationships with regulators involves proactive engagement, transparency, and a willingness to collaborate in shaping regulatory frameworks that benefit all parties involved.

Industry influencers, such as thought leaders, media, and industry associations, can greatly impact a business's reputation and market position. Cultivating strong relationships with influential individuals and organizations requires active participation in industry events, sharing valuable insights, and demonstrating thought leadership.

3. Tailoring Communication and Engagement

Effective communication lies at the heart of strong business relationships. To cultivate these relationships, it is essential to tailor communication and engagement strategies to different stakeholders' specific needs and preferences. This could involve regular face-to-face meetings, personalized emails or messages, feedback sessions, and leveraging various platforms such as social media and digital collaboration tools.

Understanding the communication preferences of each stakeholder group—whether they prefer in-person interactions, phone calls, or email correspondence—is vital. By tailoring communication channels, businesses can bridge gaps, build rapport, and foster a deeper connection with stakeholders.

Consistency and frequency of communication are also crucial. Regularly updating stakeholders about progress, industry trends, and relevant insights showcases the commitment and keeps stakeholders engaged and informed. Additionally, active listening and soliciting feedback provide opportunities for stakeholders to share their concerns, requirements, and suggestions, further building trust and collaboration.

4. Building Trust and Transparency

Trust is the cornerstone of any successful relationship. To cultivate strong business relationships, it is necessary to establish and nurture trust and transparency with stakeholders. Consistently delivering on promises, being open and honest in communications, and actively addressing concerns or issues build trust. This foundation of trust fosters stronger collaboration and a sense of partnership among stakeholders.

To build trust, it is essential to foster transparency throughout the relationship. Sharing relevant information, clarifying expectations, and disclosing any potential conflicts of interest contribute to building trust. Engaging stakeholders in decision-making processes and ensuring transparent and fair transactions also solidify trust.

Furthermore, businesses must demonstrate integrity in their dealings with stakeholders.

Ethical conduct, fair treatment, and honoring commitments build credibility and establish a reputation for reliability and reliability.

5. Creating Value for Stakeholders

Successful business relationships are built on a shared commitment to creating value for all stakeholders. Understanding their unique needs, challenges, and aspirations allows businesses to align their offerings and strategies accordingly. By consistently delivering value and anticipating stakeholders' evolving requirements, businesses foster loyalty, customer satisfaction, and partnerships that endure.

To create value, businesses must focus on a customer-centric approach. By deeply understanding their target audience, including their pain points, preferences, and emerging trends, businesses can tailor their products, services, and experiences to meet and exceed customer expectations.

Additionally, businesses should proactively seek opportunities to collaborate and co-create value with stakeholders. By fostering a culture of collaboration, encouraging open dialogue, and embracing diverse perspectives, businesses can unlock novel solutions, improve processes and enhance overall performance.

6. Proactive Relationship Management

Building and maintaining strong business relationships require proactive management.

Regularly assessing the health of relationships, identifying areas for improvement, and taking necessary actions to address any gaps or issues are essential. Proactive relationship management ensures that relationships remain strong and continue to evolve along with the changing business landscape.

Monitoring the pulse of a relationship involves actively seeking feedback from stakeholders, conducting periodic reviews, and assessing customer satisfaction. This feedback loop allows businesses to identify areas for improvement, address concerns promptly, and adapt their strategies accordingly.

Effective relationship management also involves recognizing and celebrating milestones and successes together. By acknowledging the contributions of stakeholders and expressing gratitude for their support, businesses foster a sense of appreciation and reinforce the mutual value that relationships bring.

7. Leveraging Technology and Data

In today's digital age, technology plays a significant role in relationship management.

Beyond the Balance Sheet

Customer Relationship Management (CRM) software and data analytics tools enable businesses to gain insights into stakeholder preferences and behaviors. By harnessing technology and data, businesses can tailor their relationship-building efforts, enhance their strategy's effectiveness, and provide personalized experiences that resonate with stakeholders.

CRM systems allow businesses to centralize stakeholder data, track interactions, and customize communication based on stakeholder preferences. This data-driven approach helps businesses understand the evolving needs and preferences of stakeholders and allows for targeted and personalized communication.

Furthermore, data analytics tools enable businesses to identify emerging trends, anticipate stakeholder behavior, and make informed strategic decisions. By leveraging data and analytics, businesses gain a competitive edge in understanding the underlying dynamics of their relationships and can identify opportunities for growth and improvement.

8. Continual Learning and Adaptation

A strong business relationship strategy is not static but rather evolves with the changing needs and dynamics of stakeholders. Continuous learning and adaptation are vital for staying relevant and maintaining strong relationships. This entails actively seeking feedback from stakeholders, staying abreast of industry trends and developments, and embracing innovation to create new opportunities for collaboration and growth.

Staying attentive to stakeholders' ever-evolving needs and expectations is crucial in sustaining strong relationships. By regularly engaging with stakeholders and seeking their feedback, businesses can identify emerging trends, new challenges, and opportunities for improvement. This feedback loop allows enterprises to adapt their strategies and offerings to meet stakeholders' changing demands better.

Staying informed about industry trends and developments is also crucial for cultivating strong business relationships. This includes attending industry conferences, webinars, and networking events to gain insights, connect with thought leaders, and stay up-to-date on the latest advancements. By staying informed, businesses can position themselves as industry leaders and valuable partners to stakeholders.

Embracing innovation is another key aspect of continual learning and adaptation. By embracing new technologies, processes, and ideas, businesses can identify innovative solutions to address stakeholder needs and challenges. This may involve adopting new communication platforms, implementing automation tools, or exploring new business models that create value for all parties involved.

Beyond the Balance Sheet

In conclusion, cultivating strong business relationships is essential for long-term success in today's interconnected business landscape. By understanding the importance of relationships, identifying key stakeholders, tailoring communication, building trust, creating value, proactively managing relationships, leveraging technology and data, and continuously learning and adapting, businesses can foster strong partnerships that drive growth, innovation, and mutual success. Investing in these relationships is not just a transactional activity but a strategic imperative that lays the foundation for sustainable success.

Vision and its Impact on Business Value

In today's rapidly changing business environment, the importance of having a clear and well-defined vision cannot be overstated. A company's vision serves as the North Star that guides its actions, decisions, and overall strategy. It provides a sense of purpose and direction, aligning all stakeholders towards a common goal. A robust and compelling vision not only differentiates a business from its competitors but also has a profound impact on its long-term success and value.

1. Aligning Goals and Driving Performance:

A powerful vision unifies an organization, inspiring employees to work towards a shared purpose. Employees find meaning and motivation in their daily work by aligning individual goals with the company's vision. This alignment leads to increased engagement, productivity, and commitment, all contributing to improved business performance.

A team that shares a common vision is more likely to collaborate effectively, innovate, and deliver exceptional results. This, in turn, enhances the business's overall value by driving revenue growth, increasing market share, and improving operational efficiency.

2. Strategic Decision Making:

A well-defined vision provides a strategic framework for decision-making processes. It acts as a guiding principle, allowing leaders to make informed choices that align with the long-term objectives of the business. When decisions are aligned with the vision, they contribute directly to its realization and reinforce the organization's strategic direction. This strategic alignment ensures that resources are deployed in areas that generate maximum value, allowing the business to seize opportunities and navigate challenges successfully. Effective strategic decision-making, rooted in a clear vision, allows a business to adapt to evolving market trends and technological advancements, thereby increasing its competitive advantage and long-term value.

3. Cultivating Brand Loyalty:

In an age where customers seek meaningful connections with the brands they support, a compelling vision can be a significant asset. A well-communicated vision enables a business to convey its values, purpose, and aspirations to its target audience. This alignment of values and purpose creates an emotional bond with customers, leading to brand loyalty and advocacy. Loyal customers are more likely to choose a brand repeatedly, refer it to others, and become brand ambassadors, thereby increasing the business's market share and customer base. The establishment of a strong brand reputation based on a shared vision enhances the perception of value and positively impacts the financial value of the business.

4. Differentiating from Competitors:

In a competitive marketplace, where products and services can often appear similar, a unique and compelling vision helps a business stand out. By articulating its long-term goals and purpose, a company can differentiate itself from its competitors, attracting customers who relate to its vision.

 A well-defined vision allows businesses to carve out a distinctive position in the market, offering a unique value proposition that resonates with customers.

This differentiation not only boosts brand visibility and recognition but also helps command premium pricing and build a competitive advantage. Consequently, the business's value is both protected and elevated, as it becomes synonymous with a vision that sets it apart in the minds of customers and stakeholders.

5. Sustaining Organizational Culture:

A strong vision is the foundation for building and sustaining an aligned and positive organizational culture. It dictates the shared values, beliefs, and behaviors that define a company's identity and shape the employee experience. A vision that is well-embedded in the culture fosters employees' sense of belonging, purpose, and pride. This, in turn, enhances employee satisfaction, engagement, and retention.

A culture that embodies the vision promotes collaboration, innovation, and a focus on continuous improvement, all of which contribute to the business's long-term success and value.

6. Attracting Capital and Partnerships:

A compelling vision can attract potential investors, partners, and collaborative opportunities. When a business has a clear vision, it portrays a sense of direction, purpose, and growth potential, making it an attractive investment or partnership opportunity.

Investors are more likely to support businesses with a well-defined purpose and strategic vision, recognizing the potential for long-term returns and business value growth.

Additionally, partnerships and collaborations forged based on shared visions can leverage synergies, expand market reach, and unlock new growth opportunities, further enhancing the overall value of the business.

In conclusion, a well-defined vision is essential for a business's long-term success and value. It aligns goals, drives performance, guides strategic decision-making, cultivates brand loyalty, enables differentiation, sustains an organizational culture, and attracts potential investors and partnerships. A strong vision provides purpose and direction, unifying all stakeholders towards a common goal and enhancing the business's ability to navigate challenges, seize opportunities, and create lasting value. By investing in developing, communicating, and aligning its vision, a business can position itself as a leader in its industry and maximize its long-term value proposition.

The Perils of Cultural Misalignment

In this chapter, we will explore several in-depth case studies of companies that experienced failure due to cultural misalignment. Cultural misalignment occurs when a disconnect exists between different individuals or groups' values, beliefs, and practices within an organization. Understanding these case studies can provide valuable insights into cultural misalignment's consequences and cultural intelligence's importance.

The acquisition of a company can often lead to a decline in its performance, especially if there is a significant change in corporate culture. Here are some notable examples:

Hewlett-Packard and Autonomy:
HP's acquisition of Autonomy in 2011 is a classic example. The significant differences in corporate culture and management style led to conflicts, and ultimately, a massive write-down for HP.

Daimler-Benz and Chrysler:

The merger of these two automotive giants in 1998 is often cited as a failure due to a clash of German and American corporate cultures. This led to internal conflicts and operational inefficiencies, contributing to the eventual separation of the two companies.

AOL and Time Warner:

This merger in 2000 is one of the most famous examples of a cultural mismatch leading to business decline. The two companies had vastly different cultures and business models, which resulted in a massive loss of value.

eBay and Skype:

When eBay acquired Skype in 2005, the cultural differences between a retail-oriented company and a communication technology platform led to strategic misalignments. eBay later sold Skype at a loss. 5.

Yahoo and Tumblr:
Yahoo's acquisition of Tumblr in 2013 saw a clash of corporate cultures, with Yahoo's more traditional approach stifling Tumblr's creative and community-driven culture. This led to a significant decline in Tumblr's user base and relevance.

These examples highlight how crucial it is for companies to consider cultural compatibility during mergers and acquisitions, as a mismatch can lead to significant challenges and even failure. It serves as a reminder for business owners and leaders to recognize the importance of cultural alignment and to proactively address any cultural gaps within their organizations.

To avoid the pitfalls of cultural misalignment and foster success, businesses should invest in cultural intelligence training for their employees. This training will help individuals develop a deeper understanding of different cultural norms, values, and practices, enabling them to navigate cross-cultural interactions more effectively. By acquiring cultural intelligence, employees can learn to appreciate diverse perspectives, overcome communication barriers, and embrace different ways of doing business.

Additionally, organizations should actively promote diversity and inclusion, creating an environment where all employees feel respected and valued, irrespective of their cultural backgrounds. Diverse teams bring diverse ideas, perspectives, and approaches to problem-solving, enhancing innovation and decision-making. When employees see that the organization values cultural diversity and actively seeks to harness it, they are more likely to feel engaged, motivated, and committed to the organization's success.

Furthermore, it is crucial for companies to conduct thorough market research when expanding into new regions. This research should not only focus on economic factors but also deeply analyze the cultural dynamics and preferences of the target audience. Tailoring products, services, and marketing strategies according to the cultural expectations and needs of customers will increase the chances of success and acceptance in new markets.

These extended case studies provide a more in-depth look into the consequences of cultural misalignment. By studying these failures, entrepreneurs and managers can gain valuable insights into the significance of cultural intelligence, adaptability, and the need for ongoing cultural alignment efforts. Culture should be seen as a powerful force that can either drive success or lead to failure. Therefore, organizations should prioritize cultural alignment as a strategic imperative, actively aligning their values, beliefs, and practices internally and externally. Embracing cultural diversity and leveraging it effectively will position businesses for resilience and enduring success in an increasingly interconnected world.

76

Preserving Goodwill During a Sale Transaction

When it comes to selling a business, preserving goodwill becomes even more crucial as it directly impacts the value and future success of the company. Goodwill, an intangible asset, represents the positive reputation, trust, and customer loyalty that a business has cultivated over time. Therefore, maintaining and enhancing this goodwill during a sale transaction requires a strategic approach and careful consideration of various factors.

Transparency continues to remain a fundamental aspect of preserving goodwill during a sale transaction. Potential buyers are eager to gain a comprehensive understanding of the true value and potential risks associated with the business they are acquiring. By providing accurate and complete financial statements, the selling party can instill trust in the buyer, ensuring transparency and openness throughout the process. Any undisclosed issues or surprises can lead to a loss of goodwill, eroding both the buyer's trust and the company's value.

Kevin Brady

In addition to financial transparency, it is vital to disclose any potential risks or liabilities that may impact the business. This includes pending legal disputes, potential regulatory concerns, or any environmental factors that could pose long-term risks. By honestly sharing this information, the selling party not only avoids legal implications but also establishes a foundation of trust with the buyer. Transparency builds confidence and safeguards the goodwill that has been built over the years.

Open and effective communication is equally valuable when it comes to preserving goodwill during a sale transaction. By maintaining open lines of communication, both the selling party and the buyer can address questions, concerns, and any potential issues in a prompt and efficient manner. Frequent updates and clear communication help foster trust and ensure a smooth transition. Timely and transparent communication also demonstrates professionalism and commitment to preserving the goodwill of the business.

Beyond the Balance Sheet

While financial transparency and communication are key, employee retention plays a pivotal role in maintaining goodwill during a sale transaction. Employees contribute significantly to the reputation, culture, and customer relationships that shape a business's goodwill. Losing key employees during the sale process can have detrimental effects, potentially leading to a decline in customer trust and a damaged reputation. To prevent such outcomes, ensuring that the buyer understands the value of retaining the existing workforce is important. A transition plan should be implemented to facilitate knowledge transfer, provide reassurance to the employees, and ensure a seamless transfer of responsibilities.

Preserving goodwill also necessitates considering the impact of the sale on customers and suppliers. These stakeholders have established relationships with the business and are integral to its success. Their satisfaction and continued support contribute to the goodwill of the company. Consequently, it is crucial to work closely with the buyer to address any possible concerns or disruptions that might arise during the sale process.

Beyond the Balance Sheet

By providing reassurance and maintaining open communication, both the selling party and the buyer can secure the confidence and loyalty of customers and suppliers, safeguarding the goodwill that the business has garnered.

Culture, often overlooked during the sale process, is a significant aspect tied to a business's goodwill. The existing culture not only influences employee morale but also affects customer perception and loyalty. A sudden and drastic change in culture following the sale can disrupt the business's reputation and compromise goodwill. Therefore, the buyer should be aware of and appreciate the existing culture, making efforts to preserve and nurture it during the transition. By integrating the buyer's vision with the existing culture, the business can maintain its identity and, in turn, preserve its goodwill.

Moreover, legal considerations should not be overlooked when preserving goodwill during a sale transaction. Enlisting the guidance of legal professionals experienced in mergers and acquisitions is crucial to ensure that all aspects of the transaction comply with the law and protect the interests of both parties. This includes conducting thorough due diligence, drafting comprehensive and binding agreements, and addressing any potential post-sale disputes in an efficient and fair manner. By prioritizing legal compliance and risk mitigation, the selling party and the buyer can work together to safeguard the goodwill of the business.

Furthermore, thorough financial analysis and valuation can aid in preserving goodwill during a sale transaction. Accurate and comprehensive financial reporting lets the buyer assess the business's financial health and growth potential. Engaging the expertise of financial professionals, such as accountants and business valuation experts, can objectively evaluate the business's assets, liabilities, and potential future earnings.

Beyond the Balance Sheet

A thorough understanding of the financial aspects protects the buyer's interests and helps preserve the goodwill associated with the business.

Beyond financial and legal considerations, the intangible aspects that make up a business's goodwill must not be overlooked. These include brand reputation, customer relationships, market position, and intellectual property. Demonstrating the value, strong customer loyalty, and unique market position of the business can enhance the buyer's perception of its goodwill. Additionally, protecting intellectual property rights, such as patents, trademarks, and copyrights, is vital in preserving the goodwill associated with innovative products or services.

Preserving goodwill during a sale transaction is vital to ensuring the continued success and value of a business. Transparency, open communication, employee retention, customer and supplier relationships, cultural preservation, legal compliance, financial analysis, and safeguarding intangibles are all critical components that contribute to the process.

By prioritizing these factors, the selling party and the buyer can work together to seamlessly transition ownership while upholding the goodwill earned by the business. Ultimately, this commitment to preserving goodwill sets the stage for the business's long-term prosperity under new ownership.

84

Conclusions and Key Takeaways for Entrepreneurs and Acquirers

Throughout this book, we explored the multifaceted world of business valuation, unraveled its intricate components, and shed light on the elusive factors contributing to a company's worth. Our journey has unveiled the paramount importance of goodwill and reputation in driving business value, underscored the profound role of culture and strong business relationships in shaping sustained success, and highlighted the significance of strategic decision-making guided by a clear vision.

For entrepreneurs, an in-depth understanding of the factors that drive business valuation is not just a luxury, but a necessity. It is the foundation upon which strategic decision-making is built, enabling them to navigate the complexities of maintaining and enhancing goodwill and reputation.

Beyond the Balance Sheet

Exceptional customer service, consistent product quality, and ethical business practices are all crucial elements in building a robust reputation. Entrepreneurs must recognize the enduring benefits of consistently investing in these aspects as they form the bedrock for sustainable growth and increased business value.

An essential aspect for entrepreneurs to consider is the power of differentiation. In a competitive marketplace, businesses must find ways to stand out and carve a unique space for themselves. Differentiation can be achieved through innovation, offering distinct features or solutions, superior service, or catering to niche markets. By effectively differentiating their offerings, entrepreneurs enhance their reputation and increase the perceived value of their products or services.

Furthermore, entrepreneurs should place a strong emphasis on cultivating a unique company culture that aligns with their vision. A positive and inclusive culture not only fosters employee engagement and motivation but also leads to increased productivity and innovation.

Moreover, a well-defined culture helps to attract and retain top talent, as employees are drawn to organizations that share their values and provide an environment conducive to personal and professional growth. By fostering a positive culture, entrepreneurs not only enhance the overall value of their business but also ensure a cohesive workforce that shares their vision and drives the company forward.

In the digital age, the significance of online presence and reputation cannot be overstated.

Entrepreneurs must proactively manage their online reputation, actively engaging with customers through various digital channels, responding to feedback, and addressing grievances. Online reviews, social media mentions, and customer satisfaction ratings significantly influence public perception and can reshape a company's reputation.

Entrepreneurs must prioritize establishing a positive online presence, leveraging digital platforms to showcase their expertise, build trust, and enhance their credibility.

Similarly, acquirers can greatly benefit from a meticulous assessment of the goodwill and reputation of a target company. These intangible assets are instrumental in establishing market positioning, customer loyalty, and brand recognition. When acquiring a business, considering the target company's reputation and goodwill is crucial for post-acquisition success. Acquirers should closely evaluate the reputation of the business and the industry it operates in, analyzing customer satisfaction ratings, online reviews, and other relevant metrics. By leveraging and augmenting the target company's existing goodwill, acquirers can gain a significant competitive advantage and expedite their market penetration.

Furthermore, acquirers need to pay attention to cultural compatibility and the strength of existing business relationships. Cultural misalignment can create formidable integration challenges and hinder the success of post-acquisition efforts. By considering the compatibility of cultures and recognizing the value of shared values and goals, acquirers can mitigate potential roadblocks and maximize the synergistic potential of the merger or acquisition.

Similarly, assessing the strength of business relationships and partnerships is vital, as these connections often underpin revenue streams and contribute to a company's overall value. Nurturing and maintaining these relationships should be a priority for acquirers as they integrate and optimize the newly acquired business.

To truly grasp the intricacies of business valuation, it is essential to draw insights from the case studies of companies that failed due to cultural misalignments or neglecting the significance of goodwill and reputation. Learning from these failures helps entrepreneurs and acquirers recognize the necessity of prioritizing these intangible assets in their business strategies.

In conclusion, a comprehensive understanding of the intricacies of business valuation empowers entrepreneurs and acquirers alike. Valuing and augmenting goodwill and reputation, nurturing a strong company culture, and fostering robust business relationships are all critical drivers of business value. Strategic decision-making guided by a clear vision and a long-term perspective is essential for both parties involved. By leveraging these insights, entrepreneurs and acquirers can increase business value, drive sustainable growth, and navigate the ever-changing landscape of the business world successfully.

* 9 7 9 8 8 7 3 7 3 5 6 1 7 *